Daily
Ins*purr*ations

ISBN: 978-1-59842-836-0

▉ and Blue Mountain Press are registered in U.S. Patent and Trademark Office. Certain trademarks are used under license.

Printed in China.
Fourth Printing: 2017

♲ This book is printed on recycled paper.

This book is printed on paper that has been specially produced to be acid free (neutral pH) and contains no groundwood or unbleached pulp. It conforms with the requirements of the American National Standards Institute, Inc., so as to ensure that this book will last and be enjoyed by future generations.

Blue Mountain Arts, Inc.
P.O. Box 4549, Boulder, Colorado 80306

Daily
Ins*purr*ations

...to help you always land on your feet

Romana Gould

Blue Mountain Press™
Boulder, Colorado

Introduction

A cat is the picture of peace. Cats live a simple life in want of few things. They sit in silence for long periods of time, finding contentment in a simple ray of sunshine. They are accepting, forgiving, and faithful, and they spread love and laughter wherever they go. Cats are tiny models for how to live a life of joy. They are the embodiment of and ins*purr*ation for the sentiments in this book.

These uplifting messages, and the adorable cat photography that accompanies them, will warm your heart and bring a smile to your face. Together they encourage you to focus on what truly matters, inspiring positive choices in how you treat yourself and others. This simple shift in *purr*spective can bring more happiness to each day and keep you moving on a path to a brighter tomorrow.

Inspiration literally means "to breathe in." Just as oxygen refreshes your body, this book is meant to renew your mind and spirit and fill your heart with hope. So cuddle up with your favorite feline, take a deep breath, turn the page… and be inspired!

— Romana Gould

Peace

Be an instrument of peace. Like an instrument carries and radiates music, make an effort to carry and radiate peace each day. Peace begins in your mind. It settles into your body, it can be seen on your face, and it can be heard in your words. This world needs peace and it can begin with you.

Acceptance

Your mind judges naturally as you work to make sense of the world. Every time you find yourself judging others, stop immediately. This is important when you make judgments about yourself too. If you make acceptance a daily practice, people will feel more comfortable being themselves around you and you will feel more comfortable being yourself around others.

Generosity

Create a habit of giving your attention, time, efforts, talents, and resources to others. This is best done without expecting anything in return. Giving often feels better than receiving and can enrich your life in ways you may have never imagined.

Warmth

Hearts should come with a label that reads "Keep Warm." Warm the hearts of others with a smile. Give a heartfelt handshake, a hug, or a note of encouragement. Use a soft, kind voice with positive, encouraging words. Warming the hearts of others has a rewarding side effect: your heart warms up as well!

Calm

When faced with difficulties, you have a choice. You can choose to explode, or you can respect those around you and proceed calmly. Choosing calmness reduces the stress of all involved, results in better decisions, and promotes longevity. Learn from the situation and move on.

Harmony

Harmony in music is created when two or more voices are in accord. The result is a richness that is pleasing to the ear. Maintaining harmony in relationships is a daily practice that is pleasing to the heart. When expressing feelings, begin with the words "I feel." Refrain from saying "You never" or "You always" and from any form of name calling, and the music of peace and laughter will soon fill your life.

Friendship

The seed of a friendship is planted when two beings find the rich soil of something in common. Positive interactions are like water swelling an acorn. Tiny roots sprout as our souls feel acceptance. When friendship is fed with kind words, attention, and love, it grows into a mighty oak, standing the test of time.

Authenticity

A perfect appearance may enchant initially, but your imperfections and a genuine personality are what make you lovable. You can make the choice to be like the stiff, wooden cat in the picture or like the fluffy, soft cat. When you love yourself enough to be authentic, others will love you more.

Endurance

The challenges of life help you to build
endurance of the body, the mind, and
the spirit, and endurance fosters success.
When you feel like giving up, remember
that your chance of achieving your goal
will get much greater if you hold on
for just a bit longer.

Love

Imagine you could fill a basket with love and scatter the love far and wide. As you picture this, you can't help but feel changed for the better. You will want to spread more love, which inevitably puts into motion a ripple of kindness.

Listening

You were given two ears and one mouth. This is because it is more important to listen than to speak. There is a difference between simply listening to people and listening with deep interest. Listening with interest signifies that you really care. When listening to someone, keep eye contact and create mental pictures to help you remember the conversation. Ask this person for updates the next time you meet.

Words

Words have the power to build, and they have the power to destroy. Choose your words and your tone of voice wisely. Do this while speaking to others and to yourself. Keep your words positive. If you need time to choose your words, remain silent for a few moments. This will bring more joy to your relationships and your life.

Self-Image

The mental image you have of yourself today is a seed of your future reality. How do you see yourself? If there is something that you consider to be less than perfect, do not dwell on it. See yourself as beautiful, smart, confident, and successful. Your positive self-image will help you to make decisions that will bring your image to life.

Retreat

Retreat daily to a place where you can find silence, even if it is for a few moments. Listen to the sound of your own breath. Be still enough to feel your heartbeat.

Mindfulness

Direct your awareness to the present moment. Keep your mind focused here; notice each sight, sound, taste, and touch. Do this often throughout your day. Mindfulness will sharpen your memory and bring you calmness and contentment.

Humility

You were given eyes, ears, a nose, a mouth, and an ego. Most of these help your senses, but your ego can make you do senseless things! It can make you think and say things like "I am much better than he is!" or "Did you see what she was wearing?" Quieting the ego is a good daily workout. Work to be humble no matter your appearance, achievements, or accumulations.

Balance

As a result of perfect balance, a ballerina
can twirl on her toes. If she leans too far
in one direction or the other, she will fall.
Life can make your head spin as you try
to balance your desire for pleasure with a
multitude of responsibilities. One way to
maintain equilibrium is to keep a list of things
to do and then prioritize that list. Cross off
items as you complete them. This will help
to create a calm balance so you can
dance through your days and nights.

Flexibility

Stretching your body every day helps to maintain flexibility. It can allow you to feel more open, calm, and confident. Being mentally and emotionally flexible is also important. Make plans for your day while being open to the possibility of change. Move confidently forward, keep alert, and sense when it is time to change course. View obstacles as chances to learn, while knowing that they are not the end of the road. Roadblocks can be opportunities to build a better, stronger, and more flexible you.

Forgiveness

If you carry anger in your heart from the past, give forgiveness as a gift to yourself. Holding on to anger is detrimental to your health. As hard as it may seem, it will make your heart a little lighter if you pray for a good day for those who have hurt you. You will feel more connected to them, which will open the door to healing.

Caring

Caring for another makes them feel recognized for their value, importance, and worth. It is a simple touch on the shoulder or a wave from across the room. It is a concerned look or a gentle squeeze of a hand. It is a kind word, a genuine compliment, or an effort to remember somebody's name. These tiny actions can have a far greater impact than you know.

Self-Care

Taking care of others is noble and fulfilling. You can make a great difference in others' lives. At the same time, however, you must be mindful of your own needs and responsibilities. Take time for a peaceful walk, a hot bath, a healthy meal, or a phone call to a friend. Work to create a balance so you are rested enough to be patient and make wise decisions. Practicing self-care allows you to give to others with your whole self.

Cat Naps

While you sleep, your body and mind recharge. Your body repairs damaged cells and your dreams help you to work out problems. Naps are a great way to keep your body healthy and young. A thirty-minute nap can go a long way in regenerating patience and energy. If sleeping is not an option, lie down and rest your eyes. It will make a difference in your mental clarity.

Wonder

Wonder with the eyes of a curious child. Keep your senses open, and allow yourself to be enchanted by the everyday world. Become intrigued by the sound of a bird. Be awed by the colors of a sunset. Savor the flavors and textures of your food. Instead of trying to make an impression on others, concentrate on what impression this world makes on you.

Faith

Your wishes and desires, when
strongly aligned with unwavering
faith, are the beginnings of your
reality. Having the desire is easy.
Keeping the faith is the difficult part.
Create a daily practice to keep your
heart and mind free from doubt.
This will allow your faith to stand
strong, creating opportunities for
your dreams to come true.

Hope

Hope is what opens our eyes each morning — hope for excitement, adventure, acceptance, stability, and accomplishment. At night, hope brings you home in anticipation of safety, joy, love, rest, and comfort. Every time you make the choice to do the right thing, you place a pebble of hope onto your path to a brighter future. You take steps toward better health, deeper love and connection, greater wisdom and fulfillment. If someone you know has lost hope, give them the gift of encouragement. No matter how dark it may seem, hope tells you tomorrow will be a brighter day.

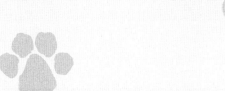

About the Author

Romana Gould is a teacher, author, and photographer. Her favorite hobby is spreading joy through photography. During the school day, Romana takes pictures of her students to share with their parents. At home, she takes pictures of her beautiful, funny cats to share with family and friends. Her greatest hope is to make others feel better through her photography and her words. She lives a happy, peaceful life with her pets and her loving husband.